```
MW00616241
```

UFOs and Alien Encounters:

Are They Real?

Hal Marcovitz

ReferencePoint
Press

San Diego, CA

About the Author

Hal Marcovitz is a former newspaper reporter and columnist who lives in Chalfont, Pennsylvania. He has written more than two hundred books for young readers.

Picture Credits:

Cover: Elena Schweitzer/Shutterstock

6: oneinchpunch/Shutterstock
10: paulista/Shutterstock
12: Index Fototeca/Bridgeman Images
18: Universal History Archive/UIG/Bridgeman
    Images
22: eflcs/iStock

26: DFree/Shutterstock
30: IFA Film/United Archives/Newscom
33: Fotografo de los Andes/Shutterstock
38: fergregory/iStock
42: © NASA/Novapix/Bridgeman Images
45: Dotted Yeti/Shutterstock
52: NASA/JSC/Stanford University/Science Source
54: NASA/UPI/Newscom

LIBRARY OF CONGRESS CATALOGING-IN-PUBLICATION DATA

Names: Marcovitz, Hal, author.
Title: UFOs and alien encounters: are they real? / by Hal Marcovitz.
Description: San Diego, CA : ReferencePoint Press, Inc., 2022. | Includes
    bibliographical references and index.
Identifiers: LCCN 2021021656 (print) | LCCN 2021021657 (ebook) | ISBN
    9781678201760 (library binding) | ISBN 9781678201777 (ebook)
Subjects: LCSH: Unidentified flying objects--Sightings and
    encounters--Juvenile literature. | Extraterrestrial beings--Juvenile
    literature.
Classification: LCC TL789.2 .M34 2022 (print) | LCC TL789.2 (ebook) | DDC
    001.942--dc23
LC record available at https://lccn.loc.gov/2021021656
LC ebook record available at https://lccn.loc.gov/2021021657

CONTENTS

Close Encounters over the East Coast

The F/A-18 Super Hornet is one of the US Navy's fastest jet fighters. It is capable of reaching speeds of more than 1,200 miles per hour (1,931 kph), or nearly twice the speed of sound. Nevertheless, during 2014 and 2015 several Super Hornet pilots flying training missions over the East Coast of America could not help but notice that, very often, airborne objects were zipping past their planes. "It accelerated like nothing I've ever seen," Commander David Fravor told a reporter. "It had no plumes, wings or rotors and outran our F-18s. . . . I want to fly one."[1]

Navy pilots who saw the objects described them as white or silver circular blurs. Each object accelerated well past their Super Hornets. Moreover, some pilots said the objects were capable of instantly changing direction, while others reported that the objects seemed to hover in midair, then zoom off like rockets. Lieutenant Ryan Graves reported numerous occasions when he saw the objects. "These things would be out there all day,"

Graves says. He adds that on one occasion in 2014, he had just returned to his base in Virginia Beach, Virginia, when a squadron mate approached him and reported a sighting. "[He had] a look of shock on his face,"[2] Graves says. The pilot told Graves, "I almost hit one of those things."[3]

Neither Graves nor the other pilots would speculate on the nature of the objects they saw. Meanwhile, investigators assigned by the navy to look into the pilots' observations were also at a loss to explain what was going on during the Super Hornet missions. Says Joseph Gradisher, a spokesperson for the navy, "We don't know who's doing this, we don't have enough data to track this."[4]

And yet there was one explanation for the sightings that no member of the US Navy would even discuss: that the Super Hornet pilots had seen unidentified flying objects, or UFOs, that had traveled to Earth from a distant planet.

"It accelerated like nothing I've ever seen. It had no plumes, wings or rotors and outran our F-18s. . . . I want to fly one."[1]

—US Navy jet pilot David Fravor

Audio and Video Evidence

Although the sightings by the Super Hornet pilots occurred six or more years ago, evidence of the close encounters did not surface until 2019 when brief videos recorded by the pilots were leaked to the media. The videos show the blurry objects streaking above the clouds as the pilots following them make awestruck comments about their speed and maneuverability. And while neither the pilots nor the navy's investigators would speculate on the nature of the objects, UFO enthusiasts were quick to suggest that the objects could very well have been flown by alien visitors. Say the authors of the online newsletter Plane & Pilot:

> The shape of the [object] looks very much like the flying saucer from popular UFO culture. And on the Navy's videos, the fact is, these crafts, a "whole fleet of them,"

according to one of the pilots, are doing things that no air-craft we know of can do. They were . . . doing things that we're not even close to having the technology to do. . . .

While we don't know what the objects are either, we do reject the idea that since they might be lumped in with fanciful (some might say delusional) fiction about UFOs in popular culture that the story is a joke. It's not. The video is here and there's something on it. We just don't know what it is. Unless the Department of Defense does know and just isn't telling.[5]

As for members of the scientific community, many of them said they were not ready to dismiss any explanations for the sightings by the Super Hornet pilots—including explanations that would

Pilots flying US Navy F/A-18 Super Hornets (pictured) have reported seeing airborne objects zipping past their planes. Video evidence of these sightings surfaced in 2019.

suggest the objects were, in fact, space-ships from alien worlds. Says Silvano P. Colombano, a computer scientist for the National Aeronautics and Space Administration (NASA), "We should consider the UFO phenomenon worthy of study . . . with the possibility of challenging some of our assumptions and pointing to new possibilities for communication and discovery."[6]

"We should consider the UFO phenomenon worthy of study."[6]

—NASA computer scientist
Silvano P. Colombano

The debate over the existence of UFOs is not new. In fact, sightings of UFOs as well as close encounters with actual alien visitors have been reported for centuries. And for hundreds of years, such sightings were often dismissed by skeptics because the men and women who reported encounters with aliens could provide no evidence other than the stories of their experiences. But starting in the latter half of the twentieth century, as audio and video recording equipment became more common in society, evidence of alien encounters could be recorded and analyzed. As a result, such evidence has gained more credibility. Advocates for the study of alien encounters can point to the sightings by the Super Hornet pilots—and the audio and video they recorded—as credible evidence supporting the existence of visitors from outer space.

CHAPTER ONE

Two Thousand Years of Alien Encounters

The first suspected sighting of a UFO was made by the ancient Greek general Timoleon in 343 BCE. While leading a voyage of warships across the Mediterranean Sea, Timoleon was said to have looked into the night sky and observed a streaking light overhead. About two hundred years later, the Greek historian Diodorus Siculus wrote of that voyage, "Heaven came to the support of his venture and foretold his coming fame and the glory of his achievements, for all through the night he was preceded by a torch blazing in the sky up to the moment when the squadron made harbor in Italy."[7]

It is possible that Timoleon saw nothing more than a comet streaking across the sky. But modern-day astronomers have traced the paths of all known comets going back thousands of years and can find no evidence that a comet appeared in the sky during Timoleon's voyage. Or perhaps Timoleon saw a meteor shower. But astronomers have dismissed that possibility as well. If Timoleon had seen meteors hurtling across the sky, it is likely the phenomenon would have been over in a matter of minutes because meteors usually burn up quickly once they enter Earth's atmosphere. Rather, according to Diodorus, the light remained overhead for the entire night as Timoleon's ships crossed the Mediterranean.

"All through the night he was preceded by a torch blazing in the sky up to the moment when the squadron made harbor in Italy."[7]

—Ancient Greek historian Diodorus Siculus

Of course, there were no cameras or other technological methods available in that ancient time to record the image that Timoleon saw above his fleet of ships. The only evidence is the story that Timoleon and his troops told of the voyage, which made it into Diodorus's recounting of the mission two centuries later. Nevertheless, since there is no apparent natural explanation for the light that streaked above Timoleon's vessel, UFO enthusiasts have suggested that the sighting could well be the first recorded encounter between the people of Earth and visitors from another world.

UFO Encounters in the Ancient World

As the centuries passed, other reports of unworldly encounters were recorded in history. The Greek historian Plutarch told of an incident that occurred in 74 BCE during a battle between the Roman and Turkish armies. According to Plutarch, the battle was suddenly interrupted by a loud boom and a flash of light. And then, Plutarch reported, a flaming object was seen falling from the sky. Soldiers from the two armies tentatively approached the object, later describing it as resembling a large, silver wine bottle.

Other accounts of apparent UFO sightings in the ancient world followed. The Roman historian Pliny the Elder recorded an encounter in 122 CE over the sky of the Italian city of Ariminium. According to Pliny, the people of Ariminium looked overhead one night and saw what appeared to be three "moons" hovering over their city. Moreover, the objects were visible during daylight as well.

A Greek general observed a mysterious light streaking across the night sky in 343 BCE. It could have been a comet or other celestial event. Or it could have been the earliest reported sighting of a UFO.

And in 776 CE, during a battle at the German city of Sigiburg, an attacking army of Germans known as Saxons halted its siege when two large circular objects suddenly appeared overhead. Frightened by the two objects, the Saxons immediately retreated. The story of the encounter is written in Latin in a history book known as the *Annales Laurissenses* (in English, the *Annals of Lorsch*). The book describes the two objects as flaming shields that hovered over the Saxon army. Says Marcus Lowth, a writer who focuses on unexplainable events in the ancient world, "Although the author is ultimately unknown, it is widely believed that writers of the time would record events as they happened."[8]

Belief in a Flat Earth

In the years to come, these types of encounters were reported again and again. In all of these cases, the witnesses—or the historians who recorded their stories—reported seeing strange flashes of light or weirdly shaped objects. None of the witnesses or the historians who recorded their stories suggested that the sources of these strange encounters were alien in nature. Although people of this period could certainly see the stars, they had no idea that other planets existed and thus never considered the possibility of other beings in the universe. In fact, it was not even widely believed that Earth was round. The ancient Greek astronomer Eratosthenes, who lived in the third century BCE, first suggested that the Earth is round, but most people rejected that view. Even into the fifteenth and sixteenth centuries, people believed the Earth was flat and that if ship captains were not careful, they could very well sail their vessels off the edge. This left little room to consider the possibility of other worlds or other beings.

But times were changing. The sixteenth-century Portuguese explorer Ferdinand Magellan, whose ship was first to circumnavigate the globe, said, "The church says the earth is flat, but I know that it is round, for I have seen the shadow on the moon, and I have more faith in a shadow than in the church."[9] Actually, Magellan did not complete the voyage; he died on the island of Guam in 1521 but his ship eventually made it back to its home port—proving it was possible to sail around the world without falling off the edge.

"The church says the earth is flat, but I know that it is round, for I have seen the shadow on the moon, and I have more faith in a shadow than in the church."[9]

—Sixteenth-century explorer Ferdinand Magellan

The Birth of Astronomy

As Magellan and other explorers proved Earth was round—and therefore a planet—many of the European world's progressive thinkers began to embrace the science of astronomy. The first telescope was made by Dutch craftspeople in 1608, but it was regarded as a spyglass. It probably would have been used by field commanders in battle to spy on the enemy from afar or by sailors at sea to scope out landing places along nearby shorelines. In 1609, though, the Italian scientist Galileo Galilei learned of the development of the spyglass. He made his own spyglass and is credited as the first scientist to aim the gadget at the sky—where he could study the stars and planets.

Galileo was the first person to see the craters on the moon. He also discovered the moons that revolved around the planet Jupiter. Galileo never suggested that other beings lived on Jupiter's moons. But the developing science of astronomy planted the notion in people's minds that Earth was not unique and that there were other planets revolving around the sun.

And perhaps there were other planets revolving around other stars as well. Eventually, plenty of learned members of society started speculating about the existence of extraterrestrial life and the likelihood that aliens could visit Earth. These people were writers, and they would help establish the genre of literature known as science fiction.

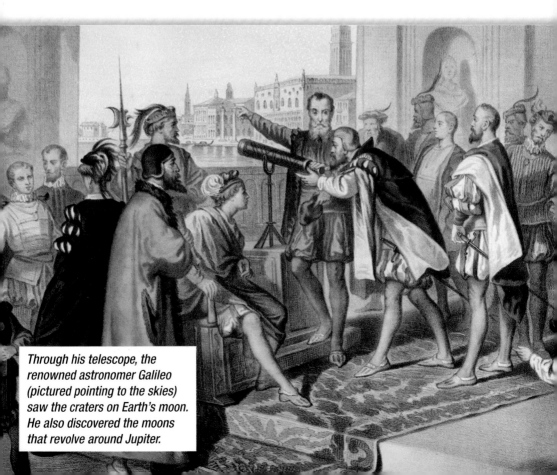

Through his telescope, the renowned astronomer Galileo (pictured pointing to the skies) saw the craters on Earth's moon. He also discovered the moons that revolve around Jupiter.

The Panic of 1938

In 1938 an acting troupe known as the Mercury Theatre on the Air broadcast an hour-long adaptation of H.G. Wells's novel *War of the Worlds* on a national radio program. Actors dramatized the invasion of Earth by Martians, the destruction of cities, and the gallant defense of human civilization by the characters in the story. Following the broadcast, a narrator cautioned listeners that the show was fiction—that no alien invasion was really happening. And yet thousands of listeners believed.

In cities throughout America, people took to the streets shouting warnings to others of the coming alien invasion. Many people fainted out of fear. Others packed up their belongings and fled their homes. In dozens of cities people jammed up phone lines to the police, begging for protection from the invaders. The day after the broadcast, the Associated Press reported, "Hysteria among radio listeners throughout the nation and actual panicky evacuations from sections of the New York metropolitan area resulted from a too-realistic radio broadcast last night describing a fictitious and devastating visitation of strange men from Mars. Excited and weeping persons across all of the country swamped newspaper and police switchboards with the question: 'Is it true?'"

Quoted in Roger Simmons, "'War of the Worlds' Radio Broadcast Sparked Fear, Panic 80 Years Ago in America, Orlando," *Orlando Sentinel*, October 30, 2018. www.orlandosentinel.com.

Science Fiction Stirs Imaginations

Actually, there had been fictional stories written about extraterrestrials and space travel for centuries before Galileo aimed his telescope at objects in the sky. In the second century CE, a Turkish writer named Lucian penned a tale titled *A True Story* in which he envisioned sailing a ship to the moon. A Japanese story, *The Tale of the Bamboo Cutter*—written by an unknown author—tells of the discovery of a princess whose home is on the moon. In the Arabian folk story *The Adventures of Bulukiya*, believed to have been written between the eighth and tenth centuries, the protagonist makes many journeys to other worlds.

It can be concluded, though, that few people read those stories. Reading was an uncommon skill, and mass printing

13

was not invented until much later. It took until 1452 before Johannes Gutenberg perfected the printing press—a machine that would soon churn out printed pages by the millions. On many of those pages, readers could find stories about aliens who made their way to the planet Earth as well as Earthlings who made their way to other worlds. For example, Johannes Kepler was a seventeenth-century German astronomer known mostly for describing the laws of planetary motion—in other words, the forces of gravity that enable planets to maintain orbits around the sun and stars. But in 1608 he wrote a novel titled *Somnium* (a Latin word meaning "the dream") in which he describes a trip to the moon.

It was not until 1897, though, that the genre of science fiction really made an impact on American and European culture. That was the year the novel *War of the Worlds* by British author H.G. Wells was first serialized in American and British magazines. The story was published in book form a year later. The novel tells the story of an invasion by Martians who make their intentions known very early in the story: they intend to wipe out all human life on the planet. The Martians show up with deadly ray guns that they use to level cities, wipe out Earth's armies, and spread death and destruction everywhere. Wrote Wells:

"Intellects vast and cool and unsympathetic, regarded this earth with envious eyes, and slowly and surely drew their plans against us."[10]

—Science-fiction novelist H.G. Wells

No one would have believed in the last years of the nineteenth century that this world was being watched keenly and closely by intelligences greater than man's and yet as mortal as his own; that as men busied themselves about their various concerns they were being scrutinized and studied, perhaps almost as narrowly as a man with a microscope might scrutinize the transient creatures that swarm and multiply in a drop of water. . . .

Yet across the gulf of space minds that are to our minds as ours are to those of the beasts that perish, intellects vast and cool and unsympathetic, regarded this earth with envious eyes, and slowly and surely drew their plans against us.[10]

From Flash Gordon to E.T.

Wells's book sparked a major interest in science fiction in America and elsewhere. Other books about space travel and alien invasions were soon published. Among them were a series of stories by American writer Edgar Rice Burroughs about the adventures of Civil War veteran John Carter on Mars. By the 1930s, comic strips were a familiar part of the American newspaper, and many readers followed the daily adventures of Flash Gordon, who flew from planet to planet as he battled the evil galactic emperor Ming the Merciless. Readers of comic books featuring Superman knew very well that the Man of Steel was actually an alien—as a baby, his parents put him aboard a rocket ship to Earth shortly before his home planet of Krypton exploded. Also during this period, the so-called pulp magazines had arrived on the newsstands. Printed on cheap paper but with glossy full-color covers, the "pulps" often featured sensational stories of UFO invasions. Meanwhile, as moviegoing became a favorite pastime for many people, the Hollywood studios were quick to embrace science fiction as well. Flash Gordon was featured in several film adaptations during the 1930s and 1940s. With the widespread arrival of TV in the 1950s, there was no shortage of shows that featured stories of alien encounters, among them *Twilight Zone*, *One Step Beyond*, and for young viewers, *Captain Video and His Video Rangers*.

An intense interest in novels and TV dramas featuring alien encounters has continued in recent years. But aliens and UFOs have found their most popular homes in the cinema. *Star Trek* started out as a TV show in the 1960s; it has lasted well into the

TV and Movies Prompt UFO Reports

In 2009 the British Ministry of Defence released a study in which it analyzed UFO reports by citizens from 1981 to 1996. The ministry concluded that whenever a TV show or movie about alien encounters emerged as a hit, UFO reports tended to skyrocket. For example, the study pointed out that in 1995, the Ministry of Defence received 117 reports of UFO sightings by British citizens. A year later, the agency fielded 609 reports. Looking at the statistics, it did not take analysts long to conclude that reports of UFO sightings rose the same year *The X-Files* (a TV show dramatizing alien encounters) premiered on British TV. It was also the same year that the enormously popular film *Independence Day*—a contemporary version of *War of the Worlds*—hit the theaters.

"It's evident there is some connection between newspaper stories, TV programs and films about alien visitors and the numbers of UFO sightings reported," says British journalist David Clarke, who writes extensively about UFO encounters. Clarke pointed out that a similar spike in sightings occurred in 1978, the year in which the film *Close Encounters of the Third Kind* premiered in British theaters. The film dramatizes the arrival of an alien spacecraft in the mountains of Wyoming.

Quoted in ABC News (Australia), "*X-Files* Linked to UFO Sighting Reports," August 17, 2009. www.abc.net.au.

twenty-first century in TV spin-offs as well as a series of films. The film *Star Wars* made its debut in theaters in 1977; the ninth film in the series was released in 2019. A very popular *Star Wars* spin-off, *The Mandalorian*, is available on the Disney+ streaming channel. In 1979 the film *Alien* was released; the sixth film in the series hit the theaters in 2017. Other enormously popular films about encounters with beings from other planets have included *The Day the Earth Stood Still*, originally released in 1951 and remade in 2008; *Close Encounters of the Third Kind* in 1977, and *E.T. the Extra-Terrestrial* in 1982. Wells's book *War of the Worlds* was adapted into a film version in 1953 and remade in 2005.

And so, since the final years of the nineteenth century, Americans, Europeans, and others have been fed a steady diet of science-fiction stories featuring UFOs and alien encounters. This has undoubtedly led many people to stare at the night sky wondering whether a blinking light or streaking meteor is actually a visitor from another planet.

The Roswell Case

In 2019 a poll by Gallup found that 33 percent of Americans believe in the existence of UFOs. It is likely that a significant number of Americans have harbored those beliefs for many decades. Back in the late 1940s and early 1950s, governmental agencies found themselves inundated with reports from people who claimed to have had close encounters with UFOs and alien visitors. The stories behind some of these encounters have endured into the twenty-first century.

For example, in 1947 numerous people in Washington State reported seeing "flying discs" across the Cascade mountain range. This is believed to be the first description of a flying saucer. It looked like a circular craft without wings or visible jet engines. Yet it was evidently capable of performing numerous intricate aeronautical maneuvers.

One of those flying discs was believed to have been sighted as far away as Roswell, New Mexico, where it is said to have crashed into the desert. The US Army quickly dispatched investigators to the crash scene. A wide area was cordoned off, preventing onlookers from gathering nearby. Finally, the army announced that the crash involved a weather balloon—a device used to observe meteorological patterns. That, at least, was the army's story. The army has stuck to that story for decades despite the insistence by UFO enthusiasts that something strange and not of this world crashed into the desert.

In the decades since the Roswell crash, numerous journalists, authors, and others have attempted to pursue the true story of what happened. Many theories have been floated, and there is no shortage of speculation suggesting that the incident involved the crash of a flying saucer followed by a cover-up by the US military. A 1980 book titled *The Roswell Incident* put forth the theory that Roswell was the scene of nuclear bomb experiments in the 1940s and that an alien civilization, concerned that Earth could turn its nuclear weapons on other planets, sent a spacecraft to investigate. But the spacecraft crashed, and the military has been hiding that secret for decades. As late as 2020, author

Reports of a UFO crashing to Earth in 1947 in Roswell, New Mexico, were initially investigated by Jesse Marcel (pictured) and others. The US Army has long said the crashed object was a weather balloon.

Sarah Scoles looked into the Roswell case to see whether new truths could be revealed. She concluded that since 1947, the US government has done everything it possibly could to hide the facts of what truly happened at Roswell. But, she claims, these efforts have largely backfired. By covering up the truth of a UFO crash, the government has kept public speculation alive. Says Scoles, "The conspiracy about the cover-up is, in many ways, due to the government's own faulty response, and it has strengthened some theorists' grips on alternative, alien interpretations."[11]

"The conspiracy about the [Roswell] cover-up is, in many ways, due to the government's own faulty response, and it has strengthened some theorists' grips on alternative, alien interpretations."[11]

—Author Sarah Scoles

It has been more than two thousand years since Timoleon saw a strange and unworldly light as he stared into the night sky. Since then, there have been many theories about what he may have seen—and what many other people may have witnessed over the centuries as they looked skyward and saw images they just could not explain.

CHAPTER TWO

The UFO Hunters

For several years M.J. Banias served as a field investigator for an organization known as the Mutual UFO Network, or MUFON. On a wintery day in 2017, Banias and another investigator—a colleague named Jesse—were dispatched by MUFON to a farm near Winnipeg in the Canadian province of Manitoba. The couple who owned the farm, Amy and Brian, had filed a report with MUFON of a UFO sighting. Banias and his colleague traveled to the farm to interview the couple, examine any evidence, and make a final determination of whether the couple had actually experienced a close encounter with an alien spacecraft.

After meeting Amy and Brian at a nearby diner, the UFO investigators followed the couple to their windswept farm. Amy gave them a tour of the farm, and then explained what she saw on an autumn morning just a few months earlier. Says Banias:

> She explained that she would always come out in the morning to feed and play with the barn cats. That particular morning, out of habit, she tossed one of the cats' toy balls

into the sky. Looking up to catch it, she noticed some-thing very peculiar—a silver round object, maybe a disc, hovering high above one of the barns, moving slowly to-wards the South. She guessed it was about 2,000 feet in the air, like a low-flying aircraft, except this one made no noise, had no wings and looked like nothing she had ever seen. She remembers ducking down, crouching low, wor-ried that it could come down at any moment. She reached into her coat pocket and snapped three pictures with her smartphone. The pictures showed nothing but an expan-sive sky and a curious blurry gray dot, far too mundane to be hard evidence. The object continued on a southward path for a minute or so until it disappeared over the barn roof and Amy lost sight of it. It simply disappeared.[12]

After speaking with Amy and looking over the cell phone pictures she snapped, Banias and his colleague concluded that the sighting lacked sufficient evidence to qualify as a confirmed UFO encounter. There was no oth-er witness who could confirm the sighting. And the cell phone im-ages were too blurry to specifically identify whatever it was she may have seen. "Nothing I haven't heard before,"[13] Banias said, as he and Jesse prepared to leave the farm and move on to their next case.

"The pictures showed noth-ing but an expansive sky and a curious blurry gray dot, far too mundane to be hard evidence."[12]

—UFO hunter M.J. Banias

Groups Dedicated to UFO Study

Although Banias and his fellow investigator concluded that Amy's sighting fell short of a confirmed close encounter with an alien spacecraft, they were not dissuaded from continuing their quest. And they are not alone. An interest in investigating UFO sightings, assessing evidence, and making final determinations on the likelihood of alien encounters has in recent years grown into a passion for many people. An international culture of UFO hunters—they call themselves "ufologists"—has been established in America and many other countries. Many ufologists have joined MUFON. Founded in 1969 and based in Cincinnati, Ohio, MUFON boasts a worldwide membership of some four thousand people—many of whom volunteer their time as field investigators.

Moreover, MUFON is not the only organization of its kind. Another group is the Chicago, Illinois–based Center for UFO Studies, which sees its mission as helping UFO investigators interpret the evidence they find. A third organization is the Davenport, Washington–based National UFO Reporting Center. The organization, known as NUFORC, maintains a telephone hotline and website that enable people who believe they have experienced encounters with UFOs to report their sightings to the organization. NUFORC does not see its role as dispatching investigators to the scenes of possible alien encounters. Rather,

Ufologists have investigated UFO sightings worldwide. One such investigation focused on a report by a Canadian farmer of a strange disc-shaped object silently hovering above a barn.

NUFORC chronicles the information it receives and makes its extensive database of sightings available to the public. NUFORC's database chronicled 7,020 reports of possible UFO sightings in America in 2020 alone. For example, on December 23, 2020, a resident of Gulfport, Mississippi, reported this sighting to the NUFORC website:

> I went outside. I always look around. And above the tree line behind my house there was a rather large ball of light. Starting from the middle of the sky. It was white and fell to the ground it seemed. Very bright no sound around at all. It scared me. I still looked trying to figure this all out. The sky in the same direction seemed to kind of light up. Then I ran inside. But it was too quiet. Not even a bug could be heard. It was odd. I live close enough to an airport and Naval base as well as [an] Air Force base but it wasn't a plane, 100 percent. Can anyone else explain what I saw please?[14]

Is Ufology a Science?

Many ufologists pore over NUFORC's UFO reports, looking for local cases to investigate, often under the guidance of MUFON or similar groups. Banias looked into several cases for MUFON. He eventually left MUFON but has continued investigating suspected UFO encounters on his own. Banias has established a website that features news of possible alien encounters while also assessing the evidence uncovered in those cases by ufologists. Banias admits that he harbors an obsession for tracking down evidence of UFO encounters and certainly understands why people develop a passion for ufology. He says:

> For some, UFOs are merely the product of fantasy and not worthy of serious time or consideration. They are a product of delusion and best served up as comedic relief. The position is held strongly by the mainstream media, for

example. For others, they are very real and of incredible importance. They drive a desire to come face-to-face with a strange and unknowable thing. The people who are driven to the UFO question form a subculture, and they shape the reality of the UFO phenomenon.[15]

Although there are many people such as Banias who have devoted their lives to investigating possible alien encounters, they often do find themselves facing enormous skepticism from members of the scientific community. The reason for that skepticism comes down to the fact that ufology is not a real science. No university in America, Canada, Europe, or any other corner of the civilized world offers courses, much less a degree, in ufology.

Therefore, many astronomers, physicists and other scientists who study the planets and stars regard ufology as a so-called pseudoscience—meaning that the pursuit of the study of UFOs and alien encounters lacks any basis in genuine scientific procedures. "Call me when you have a dinner invite from an alien," astrophysicist Neil deGrasse Tyson told a reporter. "The evidence is so paltry for aliens to visit Earth, I have no further interest. . . . The universe brims with mysteries. Just because you don't know what it is you're looking at doesn't mean it's intelligent aliens visiting from another planet."[16]

> "Just because you don't know what it is you're looking at doesn't mean it's intelligent aliens visiting from another planet."[16]
>
> —Astrophysicist Neil deGrasse Tyson

Celebrities Who Believe in UFOs

Tyson has developed a wide following and has not shied away from expressing his skepticism about UFOs. The director of the Hayden Planetarium in New York City, he has emerged as a well-known celebrity in American culture. Besides being an established scientist, he has authored several books on astrono-

Learning Ufology

Since there are no universities that offer degrees in ufology, UFO hunters are mostly self-trained. But there is help. MUFON, for example, has published *The MUFON Field Investigator's Manual*. The manual provides instructions for UFO investigators on how to interview witnesses, how to analyze photographs, and what equipment to take on investigative missions. Among the equipment suggested by the manual are cameras, compasses, tape measures, flashlights, magnifying glasses, knives, and tweezers. The manual instructs field investigators how to handle and preserve physical evidence—such as collecting and preserving objects left behind by alien visitors. Instructs the manual:

> Investigation of UFO events where physical evidence may be present offers the greatest potential for scientific pay off. It is the positive identification of physical evidence which will finally "prove our case." Although some UFO investigators and analysts have argued that certain photographs or artifacts must be genuine, the irrefutable, undeniable, scrupulously documented evidence still eludes us. . . .
>
> Our quest for definitive answers therefore dictates that we "collect anything collectible," "measure anything measurable," and "analyze anything analyzable."

Quoted in Jennie Zeidman, "Field Investigation of Alleged UFO Landing Sites," Mutual UFO Network. http://paul .rutgers.edu.

my and is a frequent guest on many popular radio and TV talk shows, among them *The Tonight Show Starring Jimmy Fallon, Late Night with Seth Meyers,* the *Rachel Maddow Show*, and *Real Time with Bill Maher*.

But when it comes to the issue of UFOs and alien encounters, there are many celebrities who sincerely believe in the existence of extraterrestrial visitors. Although they lack Tyson's scientific expertise, many of them have been willing to tell their stories to wide audiences as well. Among them is Tucker Carlson, the host of

Singer Miley Cyrus (pictured in 2019) has reported seeing a UFO that resembled a flying snowplow. Other celebrities have also spoken publicly about seeing UFOs.

a nightly news and talk show on the cable network Fox News. While most of Carlson's shows are devoted to discussing national political events, from time to time he raises the topic of UFO encounters. Carlson has interviewed several noted ufologists on his show and has made it clear that he is a believer. "We used to be defensive on this topic, but there's no reason to be," Carlson said in 2020. "There is now an enormous amount of evidence, including physical evidence, that UFOs—whatever they are—are real. Why don't we know a lot more about this? Because the government has hidden that information from us, outrageously."[17]

Other celebrities who have publicly expressed their belief in UFOs are singers Demi Lovato, Katy Perry, Alicia Keys, and

Miley Cyrus; Tom DeLonge, the former lead singer for the rock band Blink-182; rappers Jaden Smith and Post Malone; actors Kurt Russell, Keanu Reeves, Tom Cruise, Russell Crowe, Jennifer Lawrence, Halle Berry, Dwayne "the Rock" Johnson, and January Jones; model Gigi Hadid, and Green Bay Packers quarterback Aaron Rodgers.

Some of those celebrities have reported UFO sightings. In one interview, Cyrus gave this account of what she saw: "The best way to describe it is a flying snowplow. It had this big plow in the front of it and was glowing yellow. I did see it flying, and my friend saw it, too."[18] In a separate interview, Russell described his own UFO experience, "I was flying and there were these banks of lights in the shape of a triangle right near the airport. Years later, I come home and Goldie [Russell's spouse, actress Goldie Hawn] is watching this show on UFOs and the most reported one of all time was this one in Phoenix. I start to see this show and I say, 'Wait a minute, that's the night I was landing in Phoenix.'"[19]

> "It had this big plow in the front of it and was glowing yellow. I did see it flying, and my friend saw it, too."[18]
>
> —Singer Miley Cyrus

Alien Sightings Dominate Social Media

The fact that movie stars, recording artists, professional athletes, and other celebrities believe in alien encounters illustrates how widely ufology has been accepted by society. For many years books and websites have been devoted to examining the evidence unearthed by ufologists. In recent years ufology has come to dominate many social media platforms. For example, a group known as the Ufology World Research Group counts some fourteen thousand members on its Facebook page. Another Facebook group, Ufology International, counts more than forty-three hundred members. Members post news stories, videos, and other information on possible UFO encounters. Other social media

Tom DeLonge and the To the Stars Academy

Tom DeLonge, the former lead singer and guitarist for the rock band Blink-182, has formed his own ufology support organization. The To the Stars Academy of Arts and Science collects and performs its own analyses of what it calls unidentified aerial phenomena. DeLonge left Blink-182 in 2015, soon devoting himself full time to the mission of the To the Stars Academy. He explains his interest this way: "Would I leave rock and roll just to go do something that there's no data for and it's just, like, pie in the sky and we're just imagining things? No! Why would I? I mean, that's insane. But would I leave it for something that I truly think can change the world and have a positive impact and make it a better place, and something that needs to be dealt with, something that's serious?" The To the Stars Academy sees its role as collecting and analyzing evidence of UFO encounters.

DeLonge is also the producer and an on-camera participant in the History Channel's series *Unidentified: Inside America's UFO Investigation*, which has probed UFO sightings and interviewed witnesses. The series had a two-year run on the History Channel, airing in 2019 and 2020.

Quoted in Gemma Peplow, "Tom DeLonge on UFO Research: 'I Wouldn't Have Left Blink-182 for Something Pie in the Sky,'" Sky News, September 5, 2020. https://news.sky.com.

platforms have similar followings. An Instagram group known as UFO Scandinavia counts some twenty-two thousand followers. The Twitter account for UFO Sightings & News—@UFOnetwork—reports more than eighty-seven thousand followers. As with similar social media platforms, members post news and commentary on possible UFO encounters. Moreover, visitors who enter the search term "UFO" on YouTube will find themselves unearthing numerous videos of possible alien spacecraft encounters—many viewed more than 5 million times.

Many UFO enthusiasts go further than just reading about UFOs in books and on websites and posting their views on social media. Each year, several ufology-based groups stage conventions that are attended by thousands of enthusiasts. For years, one of the most popular conferences has been the Roswell UFO

Festival, which is held in Roswell, New Mexico, site of the alleged crash of an alien spacecraft in 1947. Noted ufologists have been featured as speakers and as participants in panel discussions. A key speaker at the 2019 Roswell UFO Festival was Travis Walton, who claims to have been abducted by an alien spacecraft as he was working in an Arizona forest in 1975. (Walton's story was dramatized in the 1993 film *Fire in the Sky*.) Other events held during the conference have included parades through the streets of Roswell in which participants don science-fiction-themed costumes depicting alien characters. The 2020 conference was canceled due to the COVID-19 pandemic, but in 2021 organizers hoped to resume the conference under a new name: AlienFest 2021.

One of the speakers at the 2017 Roswell conference was Nick Redfern, a British citizen and author who said his interest in ufology was sparked by his father. Frank Redfern served as a jet mechanic for the British Royal Air Force in the 1950s. During Frank's term of service, he heard many stories from British pilots who believed they had encountered UFOs during their missions. Years later, Nick says his father related those stories to him, which sparked his interest in ufology and his desire to fully investigate apparent UFO sightings. Says Nick, "The biggest challenge of all is the one that has always been there and that is the actual effort to try and find hard facts. There is nothing wrong with having a belief system and, to a degree, we all have a belief system in various different ways. But a belief system isn't the same as facts or evidence. It is an opinion or a theory, so for me, the goal is to find hard evidence."[20]

The Colorado UFO Zone

Over the years, UFO hunter Chuck Zukowski has dedicated himself to unearthing hard evidence that would prove the existence of UFOs. Based in Colorado Springs, Colorado, Zukowski often tracks down evidence about UFO sightings in rural regions of Colorado, Nevada, Utah, and Kansas.

During some thirty years as a UFO investigator, Zukowski also served as a part-time deputy sheriff in El Paso County, Colorado.

Over the years he was often called out to cattle ranches in El Paso County, where ranchers reported finding mutilated carcasses of their cattle. Whenever Zukowski was called to the scene of a cattle mutilation, he was always careful to note the exact latitude and longitude of the incident.

Zukowski then plotted the locations of the mutilations on a map. He also plotted the locations of reported UFO sightings in the same vicinities on the map and soon found a pattern: there was a definite tendency for the mutilations and UFO sightings to cluster near the region of 37 degrees north latitude. That is the vicinity of the southern-most portion of Colorado near the state's border with Arizona, New Mexico, and Oklahoma. Zukowski is convinced the UFO sightings and cattle mutilations are linked—particularly since they al-

Travis Walton claims to have been abducted by an alien spacecraft while working in an Arizona forest in 1975. Pictured is a scene from the movie Fire in the Sky, *which dramatized his story.*

ways seem to occur in the same region of the state. "A lot of cattle mutilations have occurred where UFO sightings have been seen," says Zukowski. "Either the rancher or somebody nearby would see lights in the sky."[21]

As with virtually all ufologists, Zukowski is not paid to investigate UFO sightings. And all the expenses he incurs to travel across several states in search of evidence comes out of his own pocket. Zukowski acknowledges that his travels in search of evidence of alien encounters have cost him several thousand dollars. Moreover, in 2011 he lost his job as a part-time deputy sheriff because his supervisors believed he was spending more time tracking down evidence of UFOs than performing his official duties for the sheriff's department. He shrugs off the personal sacrifices he has made in his pursuit of the truth behind UFO encounters. "With me, it becomes part of your life,"[22] he says.

Zukowski may be unique among ufologists, though, in that he is also a witness to what he believes was an encounter with a UFO. "I have not seen alien life, but I have seen balls of light," he says. "I have actually seen a craft in the sky. Something was out there that's communicating. Something was coming down."[23]

Zukowski's willingness to dedicate his life to ufology illustrates how the search for evidence of alien encounters can completely consume those who have chosen to become UFO hunters. Zukowski was fired from his job and has readily spent thousands of dollars of his savings in his pursuit of evidence of alien encounters. He believes his efforts have paid off, establishing what he insists is a zone of UFO sightings and cattle mutilations near his state's southern border. Nevertheless, Zukowski and other UFO hunters are also forced to admit that the search for hard and irrefutable evidence of alien encounters has never been easy. But Zukowski, Banias, and other ufologists will continue to fulfill their passions as they strive to prove the existence of extraterrestrial life.

CHAPTER THREE

Does the Evidence Stand Up?

In 2003 souvenir hunter Oscar Muñoz was scavenging for historical artifacts in a ghost town known as La Noria, located in the Atacama Desert in northern Chile. Eventually, he came across some well-preserved skeletal remains. The skeleton was no more than 6 inches (15.2 cm) in length. The bones for the arms, legs, spine, ribs, and skull were still intact. The skeleton appeared to be a human—albeit a very tiny human. But there was one significant aspect of the skull that piqued the interest of ufologists: it was exceptionally long, coming to a point at the top.

Physicians who initially inspected the remains suggested the body was that of a very young, perhaps prematurely born, human baby. But many ufologists declared their beliefs that the so-called Atacama humanoid is very possibly the remains of an extraterrestrial visitor. Said Chilean ufologist Mario Pizarro, "Nobody has done a serious investigation to determine what it is but I don't think it has anything to do with a four-month-old fetus. My own personal opinion is that it's something very strange."[24] Moreover, Chilean-based ufologists pointed out that the region of their country where the remains were found is also known as a hot spot for UFO sightings by local residents.

Eventually, the remains of the Atacama humanoid were purchased by Ramón Navia-Osorio, an entrepreneur from Barcelona, Spain. Navia-Osorio has used his wealth to establish the Institute for Exobiological Investigation and Study, an organization that examines evidence of alien encounters. For most of the past two decades Navia-Osorio's institute has maintained the remains of the Atacama humanoid, occasionally permitting filmmakers to feature the skeleton in documentaries about the possibility of alien life. Finally, though, in 2018 Navia-Osorio's institute funded a deoxyribonucleic acid (DNA) analysis of the remains. DNA is the molecule present in all living organisms that provides them with their unique features: gender, race, eye and hair color, the shape of the nose and lips, even athletic ability, among other traits. In this case, the DNA analysis would be able to tell whether the Atacama humanoid is in fact the remains of a human child.

A tiny skeleton with an elongated skull was found in the Atacama Desert (pictured) in northern Chile. Ufologists believe it could be the remains of an extraterrestrial visitor.

Garry Nolan, a biologist at Stanford University in California, performed the DNA analysis. And he concluded, without question, that the DNA he analyzed proved the Atacama humanoid is the skeleton of a female human child. He said it is likely the child's malformed skull was due to a birth defect and that the baby died soon after its birth. Moreover, he estimated the remains were no more than forty years old. Says Nolan:

"While this started as a story about aliens, and went international, it's really a story of a human tragedy."[25]

—Biologist Garry Nolan

> She was so badly malformed as to be unable to feed. In her condition, she would have ended up in the [hospital] but given where the specimen was found, such things were simply not available. While this started as a story about aliens, and went international, it's really a story of a human tragedy. A woman had a malformed baby, it was preserved in a manner and then "hocked" or sold as a strange artifact. It turns out to be human, with a fascinating genetic story from which we might learn something important to help others. May she rest in peace.[25]

Project Blue Book

Ufologists were extremely disappointed in Nolan's findings. Some ufologists suggested that more analysis needs to be done before the Atacama humanoid could definitely be declared human. Says Steven M. Greer, an American physician and founder of the Virginia-based Center for the Study of Extraterrestrial Intelligence:

> The bone samples provided were done so with assurances from Nolan that a thorough and objective study would be made. However, all of the [DNA experts] that have delved into his data and methodology assure me it was done at

best incompetently and at worst (and this is their belief) fraudulently. The lack of controls, the methods used and so forth were so "blatantly incompetent" that their only conclusion is that the study was corrupted from the beginning to obtain a pre-determined conclusion. This is not science.[26]

It was not the first time that ufologists have reacted so angrily at the results of attempts to analyze evidence of alien encounters. In 1969 the US Air Force disclosed that it had completed a twenty-two-year program of analyzing reports of UFO sightings. In the program, known as Project Blue Book, the air force said it examined 12,816 reports of UFO sightings and drew the following conclusions:

No UFO reported, investigated, and evaluated by the Air Force has ever given any indication of threat to our national security.

There has been no evidence submitted to or discovered by the Air Force that sightings categorized as "unidentified" represent technological developments or principles beyond the range of present-day scientific knowledge.

There has been no evidence indicating that sightings categorized as "unidentified" are extraterrestrial vehicles.[27]

Allegations of a Cover-Up

In the years since Project Blue Book was terminated, the air force has made public all the records of its investigations. Ufologists have combed through those records and insist that the air force has engaged in a cover-up. They contend that the cases investigated by the air force do provide evidence of alien encounters. For example, on December 8, 1952, an air force pilot flying over Alaska reported this sighting: "One white, oval light (which changed to red at a higher altitude), flew straight and level for two minutes, then climbed at phenomenal speed on an erratic flight path for the remainder of the sighting."[28] Another case was reported on December 24, 1953, by two navy pilots flying over the city of El Cajon, California: "Ten silver, oval objects flew at more than 450 miles per hour straight and level for the duration of the sighting."[29] And on March 20, 1966, a witness in Miami, Florida, reported this sighting to the air force: "One pulsating light which varied from white to intense blue made a jerky ascent and then rapidly accelerated away to the north."[30]

Project Blue Book includes thousands of similar descriptions, prompting ufologists to contend that extensive evidence exists to suggest numerous extraterrestrial encounters. In fact, a major critic of the conclusions of Project Blue Book was astronomer J. Allen Hynek, who served as a scientific advisor to the air force during the years in which the military investigated the UFO sightings. In 1948 Hynek was serving as director of the McMillin Observatory at Ohio State University when he was approached by officers from nearby Wright-Patterson Air Force Base and asked to lend his expertise to the air force's examination of UFO sightings. Hynek later recalled:

> One day I had a visit from several men from the technical center at Wright-Patterson Air Force Base, which was only 60 miles away in Dayton. With some obvious embarrassment, the men eventually brought up the subject of "flying saucers" and asked me if I would care to serve as consultant to the Air Force on the matter. The job didn't seem as though it would take too much time, so I agreed.[31]

Hynek eventually found himself disagreeing with the air force's conclusions. After the air force discontinued Project Blue Book, Hynek helped establish the Center for UFO Studies and published his own book disputing the air force's interpretation of the sightings it investigated. Until his death in 1986, Hynek maintained that the air force covered up important evidence in its desire to shield the public from the truth about alien encounters. For example, while interviewing witnesses himself, he found them to be ordinary people

Are Alien Abductions Real?

Over the years, many people have claimed to have been abducted by aliens. They believe they were kidnapped by extraterrestrials and taken aboard their spacecrafts. Ultimately, after physical examinations and other interactions with the aliens, they were released. One noted case involves Calvin Parker and Charles Hickson, who claimed they were abducted by three aliens in 1973 after a UFO landed near a stream in Pascagoula, Mississippi, where Parker and Hickson were fishing. According to Parker and Hickson, three legless aliens floated out of their spaceship and pulled the two men aboard, where they conducted physical examinations before releasing them.

Interest in the case was renewed in 2020 when a recording police made of their interview with Parker and Hickson surfaced. Listening to the tape years after the interview, Parker says he is struck by how emphatic he was as he described the encounter. "When I sat down and listened to it, it hit me how real all of this was," Parker says. "It kind of choked me up a little bit." Pascagoula police also said that when Parker and Hickson reported their abduction, more than fifty other residents called police that night to report sighting a UFO.

Quoted in Brian Broom, "'They Didn't Make It Up.' Interview Recording Surfaces in Pascagoula Alien Abduction Case," *Jackson (MS) Clarion-Ledger*, July 13, 2020. www.clarionledger.com.

who had experienced extraordinary events and were anxious to learn the truth about what they saw. Hynek found that the witnesses he interviewed were not pranksters, publicity seekers, or liars. Rather, he said:

> The witnesses I interviewed could have been lying, could have been insane or could have been hallucinating collectively—but I do not think so. Their standing in the community, their lack of motive for perpetration of a hoax, their own puzzlement at the turn of events they believe they witnessed, and often their great reluctance to speak of the experience—all lend a subjective reality to their UFO experience.[32]

Following the conclusion of Project Blue Book, Hynek spent the rest of his life investigating UFO sightings on his own. He maintained until his death that UFO sightings need much more investigation. He urged the US government to devote its resources to a serious examination of alien encounters—essentially, resuming the mission of Project Blue Book. Although Hynek did not know it at the time, that is exactly what the US government planned to do.

A New Governmental Probe into UFOs

In this case it was the US Navy, and not the US Air Force, that was handed the job of investigating UFO sightings. Known as the Unidentified Aerial Phenomena Task Force, the once-secret project has operated since 2007. Its original sponsor was Harry Reid, at the time a US senator from Nevada and, during the tenure of the program, one of the most powerful political figures in Washington, DC. As majority leader of the US Senate, Reid was able to marshal resources for many pet projects. Long interested in the study of UFOs, Reid found $22 million in the federal budget to fund the program. "We got a volume of research that was done, $22 million worth of research," Reid said shortly after the existence of the secret program was leaked to the press in

A former military intelligence officer who once headed the Unidentified Aerial Phenomena Task Force says he is convinced that UFOs have crashed on Earth.

2017. "It showed that not two people, four people or six people or 20
people but hundreds of hundreds
of people have seen these things,
sometimes all at the same time.
. . . I don't know what all these
things are, but I do believe that
we should take a look at them."[33]

Reid retired from the Senate in
2017, but the navy has kept the program intact. In 2020 the Unidentified
Aerial Phenomena Task Force announced
plans to make a full disclosure of its findings. In the months leading up to the release of the report, some evidence gathered in
the investigation was leaked. In December 2020 ufologist M.J.
Banias published photos of a flying silver cube on his website.
The photos were shot in 2018 by a military pilot flying 35,000 feet
(10 km) above the East Coast of the United States. According to
Banias, the pilot shot the photos using his cell phone. Sources
in the Task Force told Banias the flying cube appeared to come
within 1,000 feet (305 m) of the military plane.

After the photos were published, journalists asked US military leaders to comment, but officials from the US Department of
Defense declined to respond. In Great Britain, however, military
leaders said they are eager to learn more about what the United
States has learned about UFOs. "These revelations are extraordinary, and give the public a genuine peek behind the curtain when
it comes to how the US government is handling the UFO issue,"
Nick Pope, who was formerly assigned by the British Ministry of
Defence to investigate UFO sightings, said in a 2020 interview.
"What this new information does is confirm that the US government is taking the UFO phenomenon more seriously than ever
before. . . . I anticipate further revelations shortly."[34]

Finally, in June 2021 the report of the Unidentified Aerial Phenomena Task Force was released to the public. The report said
investigators had studied 144 sightings by US Navy pilots and

"Not two people, four people
or six people or 20 people
but hundreds of hundreds
of people have seen these
things, sometimes all at the
same time."[33]

—Former US senator Harry Reid

concluded that there was not enough evidence in any of the cases to confirm that the pilots had actually seen alien spacecraft. In one case, the Task Force concluded that the pilot had seen a large balloon. In the remaining 143 cases, though, the Task Force said it could offer no answers as to what the pilots may have witnessed. "We were able to identify one reported [case] with high confidence," the report said. "In that case, we identified the object as a large, deflating balloon. The others remain unexplained."[35]

The report spanned a mere nine pages, a fact that prompted many critics to insist that further investigations into UFO sightings need to be pursued. In response to the release of the report, US Senator Mark Warner of Virginia said he was first briefed on the sightings by the Navy pilots in 2018, and since then the sightings have continued. "The frequency of these incidents only appears to be increasing," Warner said. "The United States must be able to understand and mitigate threats to our pilots, whether they're from drones or weather balloons or adversary intelligence capabilities."[36]

Scientists Dismiss the Evidence

Although critics were dissatisfied with the report of the Task Force, the former head of the program has been more than willing to vouch for the authenticity of the evidence that has been examined and says he is convinced the evidence confirms the existence of alien life. Luis Elizondo, a former military intelligence officer, spent ten years as head of the Task Force before resigning in 2017. Elizondo has declined to be specific about what evidence he has seen. Nevertheless, he says he is convinced that UFOs have crashed into Earth and that evidence from those crash sights has been retrieved and studied by the task force. "There is very compelling evidence that we may not be alone," Elizondo says. "These aircraft—we'll call them aircraft—are displaying characteristics that are not currently within the US inventory nor in any foreign inventory that we are aware of."[37]

Although the military's interest in investigating UFOs resumed decades ago, the navy's hesitancy to reveal what the Unidentified Aerial Phenomena Task Force has found shows that government

Area 51

Since the 1950s numerous residents of southern Nevada have reported UFO sightings to authorities. Many of the sightings have been reported in a region near the town of Groom Lake known as Area 51, which is part of the Nevada Test and Training Range military training area. For decades, rumors of UFOs over Area 51 were fed by the US government's refusal to discuss what was really going on over the region. Finally, in 2013 the military revealed the truth about Area 51 after Jeffrey T. Richelson, a researcher at George Washington University, filed what is known as a Freedom of Information Act (FOIA) request. Adopted by Congress in 1967, the FOIA enables private citizens to obtain unpublicized records from governmental agencies.

Richelson uncovered the fact that the military used Area 51 to test a highly sophisticated aircraft known as the U-2. Says Richelson, "There certainly was—as you would expect—no discussion of little green men here. This is a history of the U-2. The only overlap is the discussion of the U-2 flights and UFO sightings, the fact that you had these high-flying aircraft in the air being the cause of some of the sightings."

Quoted in Jasmine Aguilera, "Area 51 Is the Internet's Latest Fascination. Here's Everything to Know About the Mysterious Site," *Time*, July 17, 2019. https://time.com.

leaders are still reluctant to declare UFOs are real. Moreover, despite efforts by groups such as Ramón Navia-Osorio's Institute for Exobiological Investigation and Study, many scientists still doubt the evidence produced by ufologists.

In dismissing the evidence unearthed by Navia-Osorio's group as well as many ufologists, scientists insist that visits by aliens are virtually impossible due to the wide gulfs of space they would have to cross in order to travel to Earth. These scientists point out that it could take tens of thousands of years for a spaceship to travel from a distant solar system to Earth. Many are also certain that no intelligent life beyond Earth exists on the planets that revolve around the sun—Mercury, Venus, Mars, Jupiter, Saturn, Uranus, and Neptune. Existing technology—telescopes and satellites—has demonstrated that atmospheric and environmental conditions on

The Apollo 11 *crew begin their three-day journey to the moon in 1969. Scientists say the technology does not yet exist for people or extraterrestrial beings to reach more distant stars and planets.*

those planets cannot support intelligent life. Therefore, if intelligent life does exist elsewhere in the universe, it would have to come from a planet that revolves around another star. After the sun, the nearest star to Earth is Proxima Centauri, which is located 4.35 light-years away from Earth. A light-year is the distance light travels over the course of a year. A single light-year is 6 trillion miles (9.7 trillion km). Therefore, Proxima Centauri is more than 25 trillion miles (40 trillion km) from Earth.

The last spacecraft to transport humans beyond Earth's orbit were the Apollo capsules that traveled to the moon in the 1960s and 1970s. It took those spacecraft about three days to travel the

238,900 miles (384,472 km) to the moon, sailing across space at a speed of about 25,000 miles per hour (40,234 kph). Although that sounds very fast, a spacecraft using that technology to fly to Earth from a distant star such as Proxima Centauri would require tens of thousands of years to make the journey.

Of course, if those alien visitors had highly advanced technology, they could make the trip a lot faster. But imagining the availability of such technology—in any place other than in a science-fiction novel or movie—is unthinkable to most Earth-bound scientists. Says Paul Sutter, an astrophysicist at Ohio State University:

> To make interstellar spaceflight more reasonable, a probe has to go really fast. On the order of at least one-tenth the speed of light. At that speed, spacecraft could reach Proxima Centauri in a handful of decades, and send back pictures a few years later, well within a human lifetime. . . .
>
> Going these speeds requires a tremendous amount of energy. One option is to contain that energy onboard the spacecraft as fuel. But if that's the case, the extra fuel adds mass, which makes it even harder to propel it up to those speeds. There are designs and sketches for nuclear-powered spacecraft that try to accomplish just this, but unless we want to start building thousands upon thousands of nuclear bombs just to put inside a rocket, we need to come up with other ideas.[38]

The lack of a viable method of propulsion is just one of the problems facing extraterrestrial travelers. How would they maintain enough breathable atmosphere in their spacecrafts for the long journey? Or what quantities of food or drink would be available to them over the course of a journey that could last several decades or more? Until those questions are answered, it is likely that scientists will maintain a skeptical attitude toward UFO sightings, no matter how many cell phone photos military pilots and others are likely to take.

The Scientific Search for Extraterrestrial Life

In late 2021 NASA was expected to launch a satellite that will carry a huge device known as the James Webb Space Telescope, or JWST, into orbit. (The JWST is named in honor of James Webb, who served as NASA administrator during the 1960s and helped launch the agency's human spaceflight program.) The JWST is a significant undertaking for the American space agency. Able to gaze into space from orbit—meaning its view will be unfettered by the hazy, cloudy, and polluted atmosphere surrounding Earth—the JWST will be able to study stars and planets billions of miles away.

Astronomers believe the JWST will help go a long way toward answering the question of whether life exists on other worlds. The JWST will not have the power to view city life on an Earthlike world revolving around Proxima Centauri—if in fact such a planet exists. Rather, the JWST will look for other evidence, such as "biosignatures" in the atmospheres of distant planets.

In simple terms, a biosignature indicates the presence of life in the atmosphere of a planet. If life on Earth suddenly ended, in time the chemical composition—or biosignature—of the atmosphere surrounding Earth would change. For example, the pollution that has been building up in the atmosphere since the Industrial Revolution in the eighteenth century would eventually recede. An alien civilization observing Earth through its version of the JWST would be able to detect this change. Therefore, it is believed that Earth-based astronomers studying other worlds through the JWST would see similar changes in the atmospheres of distant planets. And if they do see changes in the biosignatures in those atmospheres, then that evidence could serve as proof that an alien civilization did at one time exist on that planet. Says British astronomer Gillian Wright, "We've never had access to something this big in space before. To say a telescope will open up new windows on the universe sounds kind of cliched, but with [JWST] it's really true."[37]

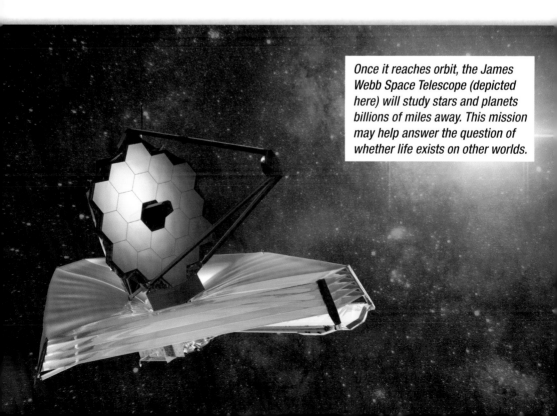

Once it reaches orbit, the James Webb Space Telescope (depicted here) will study stars and planets billions of miles away. This mission may help answer the question of whether life exists on other worlds.

The Search for Habitable Planets

Most astronomers and other scientists dismiss UFO sightings as nonsense, insisting that the sightings lack evidence of alien encounters that would stand up to scientific scrutiny. But that does not mean scientists do not believe in the possibility of life on other worlds. Instead of speculating on the nature of a blurry image captured in a cell phone photo by a jet pilot, scientists seek evidence of life on other planets. They do so by employing telescopes, including Earth-bound devices as well as those that have been launched aboard orbiting satellites.

The JWST is not the first telescope to be boosted into space. In 1990 NASA launched the Hubble Space Telescope into orbit around Earth. (The telescope is named in honor of Edwin P. Hubble, a twentieth-century astronomer who helped revolutionize the study of distant stars.) The Hubble Space Telescope, which remained in orbit in 2021, is credited with hundreds of new discoveries that have enriched astronomical science. So far, though, the Hubble has not produced evidence of extraterrestrial life. But the telescope has discovered some four hundred planets that revolve around distant stars, prompting the speculation that some of them may be inhabited.

Moreover, other satellites launched into space have made similar discoveries. For example, NASA's Transiting Exoplanet Survey Satellite, or TESS, was launched in 2018. Among discoveries credited to TESS is a planet that has been labeled LHS 1140b. That planet orbits around a star in the constellation Cetus—located about 1,600 light-years from Earth. By examining the spectrum of the light emitted by the planet, scientists have been able to draw some conclusions about LHS 1140b. Among those conclusions are that the light emitted by the planet resembles light that would be produced by a planet with a density similar to that of Earth, meaning LHS 1140b could be composed of a rocky core.

Many other planets, among them nearby Jupiter and Saturn, consist of cores that are gaseous in nature, meaning they could not sustain life because their environments are unable to produce liquids, vegetation, and a breathable atmosphere. A planet with a rocky core, however, could very well produce life—and Earth is the best example of such a planet. "This is the most exciting exoplanet I've seen in the past decade," says Jason Dittmann, an astronomer for the Harvard-Smithsonian Center for Astrophysics in Cambridge, Massachusetts. "We could hardly hope for a better target to perform one of the biggest quests in science—searching for evidence of life beyond Earth."[38]

> "We could hardly hope for a better target to perform one of the biggest quests in science—searching for evidence of life beyond Earth."[38]
>
> —Astronomer Jason Dittmann

Radio Telescopes Search for Life

Examining biosignatures in the atmospheres of far-off worlds or the qualities of the light emitted by other planets is how scientists search for extraterrestrial life. In fact, scientists have been searching for evidence of extraterrestrial life for almost as long as ufologists have been trying to prove that a flying saucer crashed into the desert near Roswell, New Mexico.

In 1960, astronomer Frank Drake altered the position of the dish of a radio telescope at the National Radio Astronomy Observatory in Green Bank, West Virginia, aiming it toward a star known as Tau Ceti, located 12 light-years from Earth. In contrast to optical telescopes, which enable observers to see and photograph images in space, radio telescopes employ huge dish-shaped receivers to listen for radio signals from elsewhere in the universe. Many dishes for radio telescopes are hundreds of feet in diameter.

Drake hoped to pick up an extraterrestrial radio signal—not necessarily an actual radio transmission of, perhaps, music or spoken words from an alien civilization, but rather sounds that would help identify the nature of energy emitted from another planet. All matter in the universe emits energy in one

Life in the Kuiper Belt

The Kuiper Belt is a region beyond the minor planet known as Pluto that is rich in asteroids. It is about 4.6 billion miles (7.4 billion km) from Earth. Observations of the Kuiper Belt through Earth-based telescopes have detected ice on the asteroids in the Kuiper Belt.

Moreover, those observations have detected the color red in those patches of ice. According to scientists, the red colors observed on the asteroids in the Kuiper Belt could be regarded as evidence that microscopic organisms—in other words, life—could evolve on those asteroids. The red color detected by telescopes is significant because it is the color that emanates from molecules that are organic in nature. Such molecules typically serve as the building blocks of life. "We're not saying that life is produced in the Kuiper Belt," says John Cooper, a physicist for NASA. "But the basic chemistry may start there, as could also happen in similar Kuiper Belt environments elsewhere in the universe, and that is a natural path which could lead toward the chemical evolution of life."

Alasdair Wilkins, "Could There Be Life in the Kuiper Belt?," Gizmodo, November 1, 2010. https://io9.gizmodo.com.

form or another. Some of that energy is emitted in the optical spectrum—thus, the images of moons, planets and stars that appear in the lens of an optical telescope. But energy is also emitted in the audible spectrum, meaning energy can make noise. Radio telescopes can pick up those signals and create a visual map showing where they originate.

Project Ozma

Essentially, then, radio telescopes listen for the sounds of the energy emitted by stars and planets. The nature of these sounds could suggest they are emitted from planets that contain similar types of energy found on Earth. In other words, the chemical composition of the atmosphere of a distant planet would emit the same type of energy found in the components of the atmosphere surrounding Earth. Says Drake, "I could see no reason to think that humankind was the only example of civilization, unique in the universe."[39]

Originally, Drake called his effort Project Ozma, naming it after the princess in the children's book *Ozma of Oz*. (Drake was a fan of the stories about the land of Oz written by early twentieth-century author L. Frank Baum, finding the characters in Baum's books to be otherworldly.) Says Drake, "What we were doing was unprecedented, of course, and no one knew what to expect. Even I, in my fever of enthusiasm, couldn't assume that we would really detect an intelligent signal."[40] In fact, despite listening for radio signals from Tau Ceti for several hours, the effort did not pick up transmissions from the vicinity of the star. Eventually, Drake repositioned the dish, aiming it toward a second star, Epsilon Eridani. When the radio telescope detected a burst of energy, Drake and other astronomers at the National Radio Astronomy Observatory believed at first that they had detected a radio signal from an extraterrestrial source, but after examining the data they concluded that the device had inadvertently detected a radio transmission that had emanated elsewhere on Earth.

"I could see no reason to think that humankind was the only example of civilization, unique in the universe."[39]

—Radio astronomer Frank Drake

Still, Drake relentlessly pursued the search for radio transmissions from deep space. Eventually, the project became known as the Search for Extra Terrestrial Intelligence, or SETI. Since Drake first commenced SETI research more than sixty years ago, many optical and radio observatories located in America and elsewhere have contributed research to the project. That research is ongoing. Founded in 1984, today the Mountain View, California–based SETI Institute employs more than one hundred scientists who are dedicated full time to the search for life elsewhere in the universe.

Breakthrough Listen

From time to time, scientists associated with the SETI project announce discoveries by the optical and radio telescopes participating in the program. In 2018 the SETI program reported that it had recorded what it called numerous "fast radio bursts" of energy originating from a galaxy located some 3 billion light-years from Earth. Said a statement issued by the SETI Institute, "The nature of the object emitting them is unknown. There are many theories, including that they could be the signatures of technology developed by extraterrestrial intelligent life."[41] Moreover, researchers at Harvard University speculated that the energy bursts could possibly have been created by transmitters manufactured for the purpose of guiding an alien civilization's interstellar spacecraft. Says Avi Loeb, a professor at the Harvard-Smithsonian Center for Astrophysics, "Fast radio bursts are exceedingly bright given their short duration and origin at great distances, and we haven't identified a possible natural source with any confidence. An artificial origin is worth contemplating and checking."[42]

Moreover, in 2019 the SETI Institute disclosed that it had discovered a burst of radio energy emitted near Proxima Centauri. The signal was discovered as part of Breakthrough Listen, a project devoted specifically to studying signals from Proxima Centauri. "It's the most exciting signal that we've found in the Breakthrough Listen project, because we haven't had a signal jump through this many of our filters before,"[43] says Sofia Sheikh, a graduate student in astronomy at Pennsylvania State University. In this case, though, many skeptics stepped forward to suggest the Breakthrough Listen team had not sufficiently established that the signal was either artificially produced or that it ema-

"The most likely thing is that it's some human cause. And when I say most likely, it's like 99.9 percent."[44]

—Executive director of Breakthrough Initiatives Peter Worden

Looking for Alien Satellites

More than six thousand satellites orbit Earth. They provide information about weather patterns, transmit TV signals, and help motorists find their way by using Global Positioning System apps on their phones. Spy agencies for national governments employ satellites to keep watch on their enemies. Many scientists reason that if Earth is surrounded by so many satellites, an alien civilization may similarly rely on satellites—which might help Earth-bound observers locate that civilization.

The so-called geostationary satellites are constantly transmitting radio signals to Earth below and to each other. Therefore, scientists reason, radio telescopes based on Earth should be able to find similar signals transmitted by satellites surrounding a distant planet. Scientists do not suggest that Earth-bound radio telescopes would actually be able to interpret the messages transmitted by those satellites. Rather, radio telescopes would pick up static-like signals, suggesting they were produced artificially by an alien civilization. Says SETI Institute astronomer Seth Shostak, "Suppose there are aliens out there who are substantially more advanced than we are. Their planet might be orbited by billions or trillions of geostationary satellites. . . . Astronomers might be able to detect this orbiting thicket of space hardware."

Seth Shostak, "Alien Satellites Might Offer a New Way to Find E.T.," NBC News, March 19, 2018. www.nbcnews.com.

nated from Proxima Centauri. Some of those skeptics even serve on the Breakthrough Listen team and have suggested the project may have inadvertently recorded an artificial radio signal originating from somewhere on Earth. "The most likely thing is that it's some human cause," says Peter Worden, executive director of Breakthrough Initiatives, the parent organization of Breakthrough Listen. "And when I say most likely, it's like 99.9 percent."[44]

Life on Mars

The skepticism expressed even from a leader of the Breakthrough Listen program shows that many scientists do not agree on the evidence that their highly technical projects have gleaned in the search for extraterrestrial life. Certainly, when scientists train their optical and radio telescopes on stars and planets located billions of miles away, there is plenty of room for skepticism. After all, these studies focus on the chemical changes in atmospheres or whether the light emitted by a planet some 1,600 light-years from Earth would suggest that the planet's core is as rocky as Earth's core.

Many scientists believe that more substantial evidence of extraterrestrial life can be found much closer to Earth. Indeed, a lot of scientific research has focused on the question of whether life has ever existed on the planet Mars—just some 90 million miles (145 million km) from Earth.

In 1984 geologists analyzed a rock found in Antarctica. The geologists concluded the rock, which they labeled ALH84001, was extraterrestrial in origin. Through further study, the scientists deduced the rock was from Mars. Evidence suggested that Mars had been struck by an asteroid some 16 million years ago and that particles from the Martian surface—including ALH84001—

Meteorite ALH84001 (pictured) is believed to contain fossil evidence for life on Mars. Found in 1984 in Antarctica, it is thought to be 16 million years old.

had been flung into space. In this case, ALH84001 traveled some 90 million miles (145 million km) across space, eventually crashing into the surface of Earth, landing in Antarctica.

But it was the chemical makeup of the rock that scientists found most intriguing. They found that crystals of iron contained in the rock had originally been produced through a biological process. In other words, a living organism—millions of years ago—had produced those iron crystals. These crystals can be regarded as fossils—albeit very tiny fossils—of a past form of life, just as the bones of dinosaurs found on Earth can be similarly regarded as fossils of a past form of life. Says David McKay, an astrobiologist at the Johnson Space Center in Houston, Texas, "We believe that these are indeed microfossils from Mars."[45]

"We believe that these are indeed microfossils from Mars."[45]

—Astrobiologist David McKay

The Search for Extraterrestrial Life Continues

The discovery of the Martian microfossils is not the only evidence that has pointed to life on Earth's neighbor. Since the 1970s NASA has successfully landed seven probes on the Martian surface. Several satellites have been dispatched to Mars as well, placed into orbit around the planet. In 2008 a Mars lander known as *Phoenix* detected ice on Mars—a significant discovery in that it is believed no life can exist without water. In 2018 an orbiting satellite discovered evidence of liquid water in existence under a layer of ice near the south pole of Mars. And on February 18, 2021, the NASA rover *Perseverance* landed on Mars with the mission to collect rock samples and soil that could provide evidence of life on the planet.

Similar missions are also under way. On May 15, 2021, *Tianwen-1*, a probe launched by the space agency of the Chinese government, landed on the surface of Mars. Its *Zhurong* rover will travel over the surface of the planet, analyzing soil and ice. It is

The NASA rover *Perseverance*, which landed on Mars on February 18, 2021, sent back this image of the planet's surface. The rover will collect rock samples and soil that could provide evidence of life on Mars.

believed *Tianwen-1*'s analyses will help provide answers to the question of whether life has ever existed on Mars. As for a mission to Mars that would include human travelers, such an endeavor is considered years in the future. According to NASA, no such mission is planned at least until the 2030s.

If NASA does eventually send astronauts to Mars, it is not likely they will encounter the evil Martian rulers conceived decades ago by H.G. Wells and Edgar Rice Burroughs. Rather, if life exists on Mars today, it will likely be microscopic—perhaps single-celled organisms visible only through the lens of a microscope.

But that does not mean the search for extraterrestrial life will cease on Earth. Scientists participating in the SETI project will continue to train their optical and radio telescopes on planets many billions of miles out in space. Moreover, ufology has grown into a significant passion for thousands of people. Ufologists will continue to examine photographs of unidentified airborne objects and exchange ideas and information with those who believe that Earth is regularly visited by beings from other worlds.

SOURCE NOTES

Introduction: Close Encounters over the East Coast

1. Quoted in Matt Stieb, "Pentagon Officially Releases Three Videos of 'Unidentified Aerial Phenomena,'" *New York*, April 27, 2020. https://nymag.com.
2. Quoted in Helene Cooper et al., "'Wow, What Is That?' Navy Pilots Report Unexplained Flying Objects," *New York Times*, May 26, 2019. www.nytimes.com.
3. Quoted in Cooper et al., "'Wow, What Is That?'"
4. Quoted in Cooper et al., "'Wow, What Is That?'"
5. Plane & Pilot, "Actual UFO Video: Navy Releases UFO F/A-18 Camera Footage," April 28, 2020. www.planeandpilotmag.com.
6. Quoted in Daily Galaxy, "'Spinning like a Hypersonic Top'—US Navy Pilots Reported Strange, Unknown Objects," May 27, 2019. https://dailygalaxy.com.

Chapter One: Two Thousand Years of Alien Encounters

7. Quoted in Jacques Vallee and Chris Aubeck, *Wonders in the Sky: Unexplained Aerial Objects from Antiquity to Modern Times*. New York: Penguin Group, 2009, p. 8.
8. Marcus Lowth, "10 UFO Sightings from Very Early History," Listverse, March 4, 2018. https://listverse.com.
9. Quoted in Ethan Siegel, "Who Discovered the Earth Is Round?," Medium, February 10, 2014. https://medium.com.
10. H.G. Wells, *The War of the Worlds*. Minneapolis, MN: Lerner, 2017. Kindle edition.
11. Sarah Scoles, *They Are Already Here: UFO Culture and Why We See Saucers*. New York: Pegasus, 2020, p. 160.

Chapter Two: The UFO Hunters

12. M.J. Banias, *The UFO People: A Curious Culture*. Guildford, UK: August Night, 2019. Kindle edition.
13. Banias, *The UFO People*.
14. National UFO Reporting Center, "Sighting Report," December 23, 2020. www.nuforc.org.
15. Banias, *The UFO People*.
16. Quoted in Lindsey Ellefson, "Neil deGrasse Tyson on UFOs: 'Call Me When You Have a Dinner Invite from an Alien,'" CNN, December 21, 2017. www.cnn.com.
17. Quoted in Tyler MacDonald, "Tucker Carlson Says There Is 'Now an Enormous Amount of Evidence' That UFOs Are Real," Inquisitr, October 10, 2020. www.inquisitr.com.
18. Quoted in Mariah Cooper, "Demi Lovato, Gigi Hadid and More Celebrities Who Believe in Aliens," *Us Weekly*, October 20, 2020. www.usmagazine.com.
19. Quoted in Cooper, "Demi Lovato, Gigi Hadid and More Celebrities Who Believe in Aliens."
20. Quoted in Christine Stock, "A Controversial UFO Conference," *Roswell Daily Record Vision Magazine*, June 29, 2017, p. 12.
21. Quoted in Michael Koenigs, "'Ghostbuster for Aliens' Investigates UFOs on the 'Paranormal Highway,'" ABC News, February 14, 2018. https://abcnews.go.com.
22. Quoted in Koenigs, "'Ghostbuster for Aliens' Investigates UFOs on the 'Paranormal Highway.'"
23. Quoted in Koenigs, "'Ghostbuster for Aliens' Investigates UFOs on the 'Paranormal Highway.'"

Chapter Three: Does the Evidence Stand Up?

24. Quoted in Antonio Huneeus, "Background of UFO Documentary's Humanoid Alien Revealed," Open Minds, April 8, 2013. www.openminds.tv.
25. Quoted in Ian Sample, "Genetic Tests Reveal Tragic Reality of Atacama 'Alien' Skeleton," *The Guardian* (Manchester, UK), March 22, 2018. www.theguardian.com.
26. Steven M. Greer, "Letter to Stanford University," Sirius Disclosure, May 14, 2018. https://siriusdisclosure.com.
27. National Archives, "Project Blue Book—Unidentified Flying Objects," September 29, 2020. www.archives.gov.
28. Quoted in Stephen Spignesi and William J. Birnes, *The Big Book of UFO Facts, Figures & Truth*. New York: Skyhorse, 2019, p. 46.
29. Quoted in Spignesi and Birnes, *The Big Book of UFO Facts, Figures & Truth*, p. 51.

30. Quoted in Spignesi and Birnes, *The Big Book of UFO Facts, Figures & Truth*, p. 65.
31. Quoted in Greg Daugherty, "Meet J. Allen Hynek, the Astronomer Who First Classified UFO 'Close Encounters,'" History, January 15, 2020. www.history.com.
32. Quoted in Daugherty, "Meet J. Allen Hynek, the Astronomer Who First Classified UFO 'Close Encounters.'"
33. Quoted in Ray Hagar, "Harry Reid Happy to Talk UFOs and Science, Not 'Little Green Men,'" *Las Vegas (NV) Sun*, June 29, 2019. https://lasvegassun.com.
34. Quoted in Keith Griffith, "Leaked Photo from Pentagon UFO Task Force Shows 'Silver Cube' Hovering over the Atlantic at 35,000 Feet," *Daily Mail* (London), December 3, 2020. www.dailymail.co.uk.
35. Quoted in Katie Bo Williams, Zachary Cohen, and Jeremy Herb, "US Intelligence Community Releases Long-Awaited UFO Report," CNN, June 25, 2021. CNN.com.
36. Quoted in Paul D. Shinkman, "US Releases UFO Report, Congress Criticizes 'Inconclusive' Findings," *U.S. News & World Report*, June 25, 2021. USNews.com.

Chapter Four: The Scientific Search for Extraterrestrial Life

37. Quoted in Jonathan Nichols, "Could NASA's James Webb Space Telescope Detect Alien Life?," BBC News, September 7, 2018. www.bbc.com.
38. Quoted in Karl Gruber, "These Are the Places (Most Likely) to Host Alien Life," Particle, March 16, 2018. https://particle.scitech.org.au.
39. Quoted in Kelly Beatty, "Project Ozma: The First SETI," *Sky & Telescope*, April 8, 2010. https://skyandtelescope.org.
40. Quoted in Beatty, "Project Ozma."
41. Quoted in Alexander J. Martin, "SETI Scientists Spot 72 Signals 'from Alien Galaxy' 3 Billion Light Years Away," Sky News, September 11, 2018. https://news.sky.com.
42. Quoted in Sky News, "Energy Flashes in Distant Galaxies 'Could Be Proof of Aliens,'" March 10, 2017. https://news.sky.com.
43. Quoted in Jonathan O'Callaghan and Lee Billings, "Alien Hunters Discover Mysterious Signal from Proxima Centauri," *Scientific American*, December 18, 2020. www.scientificamerican.com.
44. Quoted in O'Callaghan and Billings, "Alien Hunters Discover Mysterious Signal from Proxima Centauri."
45. Quoted in Carl Zimmer, "Life on Mars?," *Smithsonian*, May 2005. www.smithsonianmag.com.

FOR FURTHER RESEARCH

Books

M.J. Banias, *The UFO People: A Curious Culture*. Guildford, UK: August Night, 2019. Kindle edition.

J. Allen Hynek, *The Hynek UFO Report*. Newburyport, MA: Red Wheel/Weiser, 2020.

Avi Loeb, *Extraterrestrial: The First Sign of Intelligent Life Beyond Earth*. New York: Houghton Mifflin, 2021.

Sarah Scoles, *They Are Already Here: UFO Culture and Why We See Saucers*. New York: Pegasus, 2020.

Stephen Spignesi and William J. Birnes, *The Big Book of UFO Facts, Figures & Truth*. New York: Skyhorse, 2019.

Internet Sources

Mariah Cooper, "Demi Lovato, Gigi Hadid and More Celebrities Who Believe in Aliens," *Us Weekly*, October 20, 2020. www.usmagazine.com.

Greg Daugherty, "Meet J. Allen Hynek, the Astronomer Who First Classified UFO 'Close Encounters,'" History, January 15, 2020. www.history.com.

Michael Koenigs, "'Ghostbuster for Aliens' Investigates UFOs on the 'Paranormal Highway,'" ABC News, February 14, 2018. https://abcnews.go.com.

Jonathan O'Callaghan and Lee Billings, "Alien Hunters Discover Mysterious Signal from Proxima Centauri," *Scientific American*, December 18, 2020. www.scientific american.com.

Ian Sample, "Genetic Tests Reveal Tragic Reality of Atacama 'Alien' Skeleton," *The Guardian* (Manchester, UK), March 22, 2018. www.theguardian.com.

Websites

Center for UFO Studies

www.cufos.org

Founded by J. Allen Hynek, the scientific adviser to Project Blue Book, the center includes many reports of UFO sightings. By accessing the link for "UFO Case Files" on the website, visitors can find reports on dozens of alien encounters that include testimony by witnesses and statements by police and other governmental agencies investigating the cases.

The Debrief

https://thedebrief.org

Established by uflogist M.J. Banias, the website provides reports from ufologists as well as news of scientific evidence of alien life uncovered by observatories and satellites. By accessing the tab for "Ideas," visitors can read essays about the likelihood of communicating with aliens and whether it is possible to travel in spacecraft at faster than the speed of light.

James Webb Space Telescope

www.jwst.nasa.gov

Established by the National Aeronautics and Space Administration, this website provides the latest news on the development and expected launch of the James Webb Space Telescope. Visitors to the site can find images of the telescope and the projects the device will undertake after its 2021 launch, including examinations of distant galaxies.

Mutual UFO Network (MUFON)

www.mufon.com

MUFON counts more than four thousand members, many of whom undertake investigations of UFO encounters and report their findings to MUFON. By accessing the "Track UFOs" page on the MUFON website, visitors can find a map of the United States where recent UFO sightings have been reported.

National UFO Reporting Center

http://nuforc.org

The National UFO Reporting Center maintains a hotline and website where people who believe they have seen UFOs can report their sightings. Visitors to the website can read descriptions of UFOs reported by witnesses by accessing the "Report Database" page on the website. The database is updated daily.

Project Blue Book, National Archives
www.archives.gov/research/military/air-force/ufos

A summary of Project Blue Book—the twenty-two-year program by the US Air Force to analyze UFO sightings—can be found on this website maintained by the National Archives. The website includes the US government's declaration that no flying saucer crashed in the desert near Roswell, New Mexico, in 1947, as well as numerous individual reports of UFO sightings.

SETI Institute
www.seti.org

Based in Mountain View, California, the SETI Institute is devoted to a scientific search for extraterrestrial intelligence. Visitors to the institute's website can find articles on current SETI studies by accessing the "Research" tab on the website. Among those studies is a look at how a planet can develop the environment necessary to become habitable.

INDEX